I Can

Share with Others

Written by Jenette Donovan Guntly
Photographed by Michael Jarrett

GARETH**STEVENS**
GS
PUBLISHING
A World Almanac Education Group Company

Please visit our web site at: www.garethstevens.com
For a free color catalog describing Gareth Stevens Publishing's list of high-quality books
and multimedia programs, call 1-800-542-2595 (USA) or 1-800-387-3178 (Canada).
Gareth Stevens Publishing's fax: (414) 332-3567.

Library of Congress Cataloging-in-Publication Data

Guntly, Jenette Donovan.
  (Sharing is caring)
  I can share with others / written by Jenette Donovan Guntly; photographed by Michael Jarrett.
    p. cm. — (Doing the right thing)
  ISBN 0-8368-4246-4 (lib. bdg.)
  1. Sharing—Juvenile literature. I. Jarrett, Michael, 1956- . II. Title.
  BJ1533.G4G86   2004
  177'.7—dc22   2004045299

This North American edition first published in 2005 by
Gareth Stevens Publishing
A World Almanac Education Group Company
330 West Olive Street, Suite 100
Milwaukee, WI 53212 USA

This edition copyright © 2005 by Gareth Stevens, Inc. Original edition copyright © 2002 by Creative Teaching Press, Inc.,
P.O. Box 2723, Huntington Beach, CA 92647-0723. First published in the United States in 2002 as *Sharing is Caring: Learning
about Generosity* by Creative Teaching Press, Inc. Original text copyright © 2002 by Regina G. Burch.

Photographer: Michael Jarrett
Gareth Stevens designer: Kami M. Koenig

Printed in the United States of America

1 2 3 4 5 6 7 8 9 08 07 06 05 04

I can share with others!

Granddad brings a special treat.

We visit for a while.

He shows me all his photographs.

They always make me smile.

Joe and Debbie come to play.

I share Granddad's surprise.

We decide we'd like to draw.

I hand out art supplies.

We make a special thank-you card,

and we all do our parts.

We want to show that Granddad has

a place in all our hearts.

We feel good when we all share.
Being generous shows we care.